Love Poems

Love Poems

BRACKEN BOOKS
LONDON

Love Poems

This edition published in 1994 by Bracken Books, an imprint of Studio Editions Ltd, Princess House, 50 Eastcastle Street, London W1N 7AP, England

ISBN 1 85891 130 3

Printed in India

To A...
June 1897
G.W.E.

Dedication:
of the
Drawings:

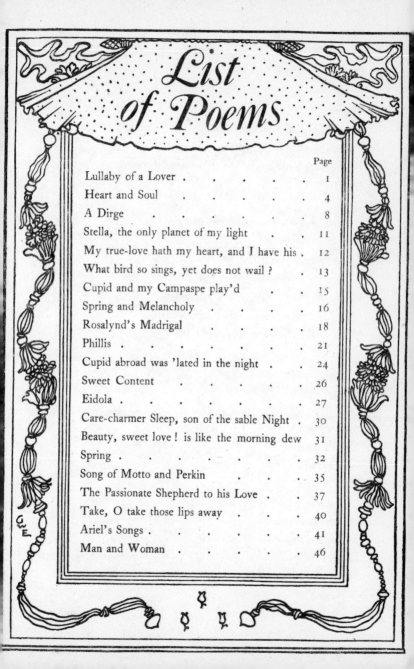

List of Poems

	Page
Lullaby of a Lover	1
Heart and Soul	4
A Dirge	8
Stella, the only planet of my light	11
My true-love hath my heart, and I have his	12
What bird so sings, yet does not wail?	13
Cupid and my Campaspe play'd	15
Spring and Melancholy	16
Rosalynd's Madrigal	18
Phillis	21
Cupid abroad was 'lated in the night	24
Sweet Content	26
Eidola	27
Care-charmer Sleep, son of the sable Night	30
Beauty, sweet love! is like the morning dew	31
Spring	32
Song of Motto and Perkin	35
The Passionate Shepherd to his Love	37
Take, O take those lips away	40
Ariel's Songs	41
Man and Woman	46

List of Poems

	Page
Spring	48
Winter	51
Blow, blow, thou winter wind	52
Under the greenwood tree	54
Hark ! hark ! the lark at heaven's gate sings	56
Fidele	57
Sylvia	59
O mistress mine, where are you roaming ?	60
Song of Autolycus	61
Come away, come away, Death	64
That time of year thou mayst in me behold	65
Let me not to the marriage of true minds	66
Shall I compare thee to a summer's day ?	69
When in the chronicle of wasted time	71
To Celia	73
The Sweet Neglect	74
The Shepherds' Holiday	75
Echo's Song	77
An Ode to Himself	79
The Invitation	81
Good-Morrow	82
To Phyllis	84
Beauty clear and fair	87
Invocation to Sleep	88
To Celia Singing	89
Hymn to Pan	90
For Summer Time	92

List of Poems

	Page
The Manly Heart	94
Phœbus, arise !	98
Trust not, Sweet Soul ! those curlèd waves of gold	101
The Song of Celadyne	104
Ask me no more where Jove bestows	107
Disdain Returned	109
Chloris in the Snow	110
Delight in Disorder	112
To Julia	113
To Meadows	116
To the Virgins, to make much of Time	118
To the Rose	121
To Daffodils	122
Corinna's Maying	125
To Daisies	129
To Anthea who may command him Any Thing	130
To One saying she was Old	132
Description of Castara	134
On a Girdle	138
Go, lovely Rose !	139
To Chloris	141
Stay, Phœbus ! stay !	142
To Flavia	143
Whoe'er she be	145
A Ballad upon a Wedding	150
Why so pale and wan, fond lover ?	156
Constancy	157

List of Poems

	Page
I prithee send me back my heart	158
To Althea from Prison	161
To Lucasta, going beyond the Seas	164
To Lucasta, on going to the Wars	166
The Grasshopper	167
Cherry Ripe	169
Though you are young, and I am old	172
Amarillis	173
Where she her sacred bower adorns	176
The man of life upright	179
The peaceful western wind	181
My sweetest Lesbia, let us live and love	183
Night as well as brightest day hath her delight	186

List of Drawings

Lullaby of a Lover	*opp. page*	1
Heart and Soul		4
Cupid and my Campaspe		15
Cupid abroad was 'lated in the night		22
Eidola		29
Spring		32
The Passionate Shepherd		39
Ariel's Songs		43
Ariel's Songs		45
Man and Woman		46
Winter		51
Under the greenwood tree		54
The Song of Autolycus		63
Let me not to the union of true minds		66
Echo's Song		79
To Phyllis		84
Hymn to Pan		90
The Manly Heart		94
Trust not		103
Chloris in the Snow		110
To Julia		115
Gather ye rosebuds while ye may		118
Corinna's Maying		125
On a Girdle		136
Whoe'er she be		147
I prithee send me back my heart		158
To Althea from Prison		163
Cherry Ripe		171
Amarillis		175
My sweetest Lesbia		185

Lullaby of a Lover

SING lullaby, as women do
  With which they bring their babes to rest;
And lullaby can I sing too,
  As womanly as can the best.
With lullaby they still the child;
And if I be not much beguiled,
Full many wanton babes have I
Which must be stilled with lullaby.

First, lullaby my youthful years;
  It is now time to go to bed,
For crooked age and hoary hairs,
  Have now the haven within my head.

[1]

Lullaby of a Lover

With lullaby then Youth be still,
With lullaby content thy will;
Since courage quails, and come behind;
Go, sleep! and so beguile thy mind.

Next, lullaby my gazing Eyes,
    Which wonted were to glance apace;
For every glass may now suffice
    To show the furrows in my face.
With lullaby then wink awhile,
With lullaby your looks beguile;
Let no fair face, or beauty bright,
Entice you eft with vain delight.

And lullaby my wanton Will,
    Let Reason's rule now rein my thought,
Since all too late I find by skill
    How dear I have thy fancies bought.
With lullaby now take thine ease,
With lullaby thy doubt appease;
For trust in this, — if thou be still,
My body shall obey thy will.

Thus lullaby my Youth, mine Eyes,
  My Will, my ware and all that was,
I can no more delays devise,
  But welcome pain, let pleasure pass.
With lullaby now take you leave,
With lullaby your dreams deceive;
And when you rise with waking eye,
Remember then this lullaby.

— George Gascoigne.

Heart and Soul

O FAIR! O sweet! when I do look on thee,
In whom all joys so well agree,
Heart and soul do sing in me.
This you hear is not my tongue,
Which once said what I conceivèd,
For it was of use bereavèd,
With a cruel answer strong.
No; though tongue to roof be cleavèd,
Fearing lest he chastised be,
Heart and soul do sing in me.

O fair! O sweet! when I do look on thee,
In whom all joys so well agree,
Heart and soul do sing in me.
Just accord all music makes;

In thee just accord excelleth,
Where each part in such peace dwelleth,
  One of other, beauty takes.
Since, then, truth to all minds telleth
  That in thee lives harmony,
    Heart and soul do sing in me.

O fair! O sweet! when I do look on thee,
  In whom all joys so well agree,
Heart and soul do sing in me.
  They that heaven have known do say,
That whoso that grace obtaineth,
To see what fair sight there reigneth,
  Forcèd are to sing alway:
So then, since that heaven remaineth
  In thy face I plainly see,
    Heart and soul do sing in me.

O fair! O sweet! when I do look on thee,
  In whom all joys so well agree,
Heart and soul do sing in me.
  Sweet, think not I am at ease,

For because my chief part singeth;
This song from death's sorrow springeth,
  As to swan in last disease:
For no dumbness nor death bringeth
  Stay to true love's melody:
  Heart and soul do sing in me.

—*Sir Philip Sidney.*

A Dirge

RING out your bells, let mourning shows
　　be spread.
　　For love is dead:
　　　All Love is dead, infected
With plague of deep disdain;
　　Worth, as naught worth, rejected,
And faith fair scorn doth gain.
　　From so ungrateful fancy,
　　From such a female frenzy,
　　From them that use men thus,
　　Good Lord, deliver us!

Weep, neighbours, weep; do you not hear it
　　said
That Love is dead?

A Dirge

His deathbed, peacock's Folly;
His winding sheet is Shame;
  His will, False Seeming wholly;
His sole executor, Blame.
  From so ungrateful fancy,
  From such a female frenzy,
  From them that use men thus,
  Good Lord, deliver us!

Let dirge be sung, and trentals rightly read,
For Love is dead;
  Sir Wrong his tomb ordaineth
My mistress' marble heart;
  Which epitaph containeth,
'Her eyes were once his dart.'
  From so ungrateful fancy,
  From such a female frenzy,
  From them that use men thus,
  Good Lord, deliver us!

Alas, I lie; rage hath this error bred;
Love is not dead;
  Love is not dead, but sleepeth,
In her unmatchèd mind,

A Dirge

Where she his counsel keepeth,
Till due deserts she find.
Therefore from so vile fancy,
To call such wit a frenzy,
Who Love can temper thus,
Good Lord, deliver us.

— Sir Philip Sidney.

STELLA, the only planet of my light,
Light of my life, and life of my desire,
Chief good whereto my hope doth only 'spire,
World of my wealth, and heav'n of my delight;
Why dost thou spend the treasure of thy spite
With voice more fit to wed Amphion's lyre,
Seeking to quench in me the noble fire
Fed by thy worth, and kindled by thy sight?
And all in vain: for while thy breath most sweet
With choicest words, thy words with reasons rare,
Thy reasons firmly set on Virtue's feet,
Labor to kill in me this killing care
O think I then, what paradise of joy
It is, so fair a virtue to enjoy!

— *Sir Philip Sidney.*

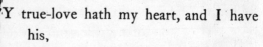

Y true-love hath my heart, and I have
   his,
   By just exchange one for another
    given:
I hold his dear, and mine he cannot
   miss,
There never was a better bargain driven:
   My true-love hath my heart, and I
    have his.

His heart in me keeps him and me in
   one,
My heart in him his thoughts and senses guides:
He loves my heart, for once it was his own,
I cherish his because in me it bides:
   My true-love hath my heart, and I have his.

                   — *Sir Philip Sidney.*

WHAT bird so sings, yet does so wail?
O 'tis the ravished nightingale.
"Jug, jug, jug, jug, teren," she
    cries,
And still her woes at midnight rise.
Brave prick song! who is't now we
    hear?
None but the lark so shrill and clear;
Now at heaven's gates she claps her
    wings,
The morn not waking till she sings.
Hark! hark! with what a pretty throat
Poor robin redbreast tunes his note;
Hark how the jolly cuckoo sing,
Cuckoo to welcome in the spring;
Cuckoo to welcome in the spring!

— *John Lyly.*

GEORGE WHARTON EDWARDS · MARCH · MDCCCXCVII ·

CUPID and my Campaspe play'd
    At cards for kisses; Cupid paid:
    He stakes his quiver, bow, and
        arrows,
His mother's doves, and team of spar-
        rows;
Loses them too; then down he throws
The coral of his lip, the rose
Growing on's cheek (but none knows
        how);
With these, the crystal of his brow,
And then the dimple on his chin;
All these did my Campaspe win:
And last he set her both his eyes —
She won, and Cupid blind did rise.
    O Love, has she done this to thee?
    What shall, alas! become of me?
                        — *John Lyly.*

Spring and Melancholy

THE earth, late choked with showers,
Is now arrayed in green;
Her bosom springs with flowers,
The air dissolves her teen;
  The heavens laugh at her glory:
  Yet bide I sad and sorry.

The woods are decked with leaves,
And trees are clothed gay;
And Flora crowned with sheaves
With oaken boughs doth play,
  Where I am clad in black
  In token of my wrack.

Spring and Melancholy

The birds upon the trees
Do sing with pleasant voices,
And chant in their degrees
Their loves and lucky choices;
　　When I, whilst they are singing,
　　With sighs mine arms am wringing.

The thrushes seek the shade,
And I my fatal grave;
Their flight to heaven is made,
My walk on earth I have;
　　They free, I thrall; they jolly,
　　I sad and pensive wholly.

— Thomas Lodge.

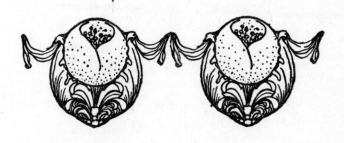

Rosalynd's Madrigal

Love in my bosom, like a bee,
    Doth suck his sweet;
Now with his wings he plays with me,
    Now with his feet.
  Within mine eyes he makes his nest,
  His bed amidst my tender breast;
  My kisses are his daily feast,
  And yet he robs me of my rest:
    Ah! wanton, will ye?

And if I sleep, then percheth he
    With pretty flight,
And makes his pillow of my knee
    The livelong night.

Strike I my lute, he tunes the string;
He music plays if so I sing;
He lends me every lovely thing,
Yet cruel he my heart doth sting:
    Whist, wanton, will ye?

Else I with roses every day
    Will whip you hence,
And bind you, when you long to play,
    For your offence;
I'll shut my eyes to keep you in;
I'll make you fast it for your sin;
I'll count your power not worth a pin;
— Alas! what hereby shall I win,
    If he gainsay me?

What if I beat the wanton boy
    With many a rod?
He will repay me with annoy,
    Because a god.
Then sit thou safely on my knee,

And let thy bower my bosom be;
Lurk in mine eyes, I like of thee,
O Cupid! so thou pity me,
　　Spare not, but play thee!

— *Thomas Lodge.*

Phillis

OVE guards the roses of thy lips,
   And flies about them like a bee:
If I approach he forward skips,
   And if I kiss he stingeth me.

Love in thine eyes doth build his
      bower,
   And sleeps within their pretty shine;
And if I look the boy will lour,
   And from their orbs shoots shafts
      divine.

Love works thy heart within his fire,
   And in my tears doth firm the
      same;
And if I tempt it will retire,
   And of my plaints doth make a
      game.

[21]

Phillis

Love! let me cull her choicest flowers,
　And pity me, and calm her eye!
Make soft her heart! dissolve her lours!
　Then will I praise thy deity.
But if thou do not, Love! I'll truly serve her
In spite of thee, and by firm faith deserve her.

— Thomas Lodge.

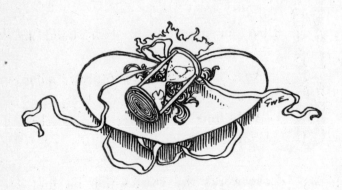

~ GEORGE WHARTON EDWARDS ~

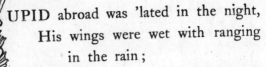

CUPID abroad was 'lated in the night,
   His wings were wet with ranging
      in the rain;
   Harbour he sought: to me he took
      his flight
To dry his plumes. I heard the boy
      complain;
   I oped the door, and granted his
      desire;
   I rose myself, and made the wag a
      fire.

Looking more narrow, by the fire's flame,
   I spied his quiver hanging by his back;
Doubting the boy might my misfortune frame,
   I would have gone, for fear of further
      wrack;
      But what I dread, did me, poor wretch,
         betide,
      For forth he drew an arrow from his side.

[24]

" Cupid abroad was 'lated in the night "

He pierced the quick, and I began to start:
  A pleasing wound, but that it was too high;
His shaft procured a sharp, yet sugared smart.
  Away he flew, for why, his wings were dry;
    And left the arrow sticking in my breast,
    That sore I grieved I welcomed such a guest.

— *Robert Greene.*

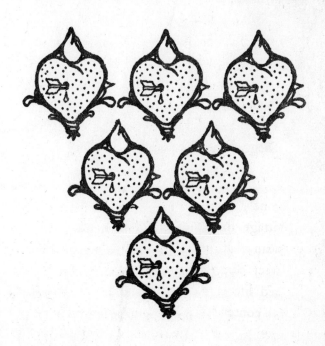

Sweet Content

SWEET are the thoughts that savour
of content;
The quiet mind is richer than a
crown;
Sweet are the nights in careless slumber
spent;
The poor estate scorns Fortune's angry
frown:
Such sweet content, such minds, such
sleep, such bliss,
Beggars enjoy, when princes oft do
miss.

The homely house that harbours quiet rest,
The cottage that affords nor pride nor care,
The mean that 'grees with country music best,
The sweet consort of mirth and modest fare, —
Obscurèd life sets down a type of bliss:
A mind content both crown and kingdom is.

— *Robert Greene.*

Eidola

Are they shadows that we see?
And can shadows pleasure give?
Pleasures only shadows be,
Cast by bodies we conceive,
And are made the things we deem
In those figures which they seem.

But these pleasures vanish fast
Which by shadows are exprest;
Pleasures are not if they last,
In their passage is their best:
Glory is most bright and gay
In a flash and so away.

Feed apace then, greedy eyes,
On the wonder you behold;
Take it sudden as it flies,
Though you take it not to hold:
When your eyes have done their part,
Thought must length it in the heart.

— *Samuel Daniel.*

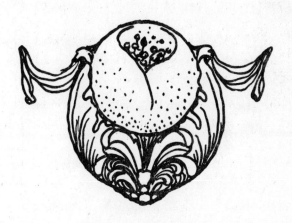

CARE-CHARMER Sleep, son of the
      sable Night,
    Brother to Death, in silent dark-
      ness born,
Relieve my languish, and restore the light;
With dark forgetting of my care return.

And let the day be time enough to mourn
The shipwreck of my ill-adventured
      youth:
Let waking eyes suffice to wail their scorn,
Without the torment of the night's untruth.

Cease, dreams, the images of day-desires,
To model forth the passions of the morrow;
Never let rising Sun approve you liars,
To add more grief to aggravate my sorrow:

Still let me sleep, embracing clouds in vain,
And never wake to feel the day's disdain.

—*Samuel Dàniel.*

[30]

BEAUTY, sweet love! is like the
morning dew,
Whose short refresh upon the
tender green,
Cheers for a time, but still the sun doth
show
And straight is gone as it had never
been.
Soon doth it fade that makes the fairest
flourish;
Short is the glory of the blushing
rose,—
The hue which thou so carefully dost nourish
Yet which at length thou must be forced to
lose;
When thou, surcharged with burthen of thy years,
Shalt bend thy wrinkles homeward to the
earth,
And that in Beauty's lease expired appears,
The date of age, the kalends of our dearth;—
But ah, no more! this must not be foretold;
For women grieve to think they must be old.

—Samuel Daniel.

Spring

Spring, the sweet Spring, is the year's pleasant
    king;
Then blooms each thing, then maids dance in
    a ring,
Cold doth not sting, the pretty birds do
    sing,
   Cuckoo, jug-jug, pu-we, to-witta-woo!

The palm and may make country houses gay,
Lambs frisk and play, the shepherds pipe all
    day,
And we hear aye birds tune this merry lay,
   Cuckoo, jug-jug, put, we-o-witta-woo.

GEORGE WHARTON EDWARDS

Spring

The fields breathe sweet, the daisies kiss our
      feet,
Young lovers meet, old wives a-sunning sit,
In every street these tunes our ears do greet,
    Cuckoo, jug-jug, pu-we, to-witta-woo!
      Spring! the sweet Spring!

— Thomas Nash.

Song of Motto and Perkin

Motto. TELL me, thou skilful shepherd swain!
        Who's yonder in the valley set?
Perkin. O, it is She whose sweets do stain
        The lily, rose, the violet.

Motto. Why doth the Sun against his kind,
        Stay his bright chariot in the skies?
Perkin. He pauseth almost stricken blind
        With gazing on her heavenly eyes.

Motto. Why do the flocks forbear their food
        Which sometime was their chief delight?
Perkin. Because they need no other good
        That live in presence of her sight.

Motto. How come these flowers to flourish still,
Not withering with sharp Winter's death?
Perkin. She hath robb'd Nature of her skill,
And comforts all things with her breath.

Motto. Why slide these brooks so slow away,
As swift as the wild roe that were?
Perkin. O, muse not, shepherd! that they stay,
When they her heavenly voice do hear.

Motto. From whence come all these goodly
swains
And lovely girls attired in green?
Perkin. From gathering garlands on the plains
To crown thy Syl; our shepherd's Queen.

The sun that lights this world below,
Flocks, brooks, and flowers can witness bear,
These shepherds and these nymphs do know,
That Sylvia is as chaste as fair.

— *Michael Drayton.*

The Passionate Shepherd to his Love

Come live with me and be my Love,
And we will all the pleasures prove
That hills and valleys, dale and field,
And all the craggy mountains yield.

There will we sit upon the rocks
And see the shepherds feed their flocks,
By shallow rivers, to whose falls
Melodious birds sing madrigals.

There will I make thee beds of roses
And a thousand fragrant posies,
A cap of flowers, and a kirtle
Embroider'd all with leaves of myrtle.

[37]

GEORGE WHARTON EDWARDS

A gown made of the finest wool,
Which from our pretty lambs we pull,
Fair lined slippers for the cold,
With buckles of the purest gold.

A belt of straw and ivy buds
With coral clasps and amber studs:
And if these pleasures may thee move,
Come live with me and be my Love.

Thy silver dishes for thy meat
As precious as the gods do eat,
Shall on an ivory table be
Prepared each day for thee and me.

The shepherd swains shall dance and sing
For thy delight each May-morning:
If these delights thy mind may move,
Then live with me and be my Love.

— Christopher Marlowe.

TAKE, O take those lips away
That so sweetly were forsworn,
And those eyes, like break of day,
Lights that do mislead the morn:
But my kisses bring again,
        Bring again —
Seals of love, but seal'd in vain,
        Seal'd in vain!

                        — *William Shakespeare.*

Ariel's Songs

I

WHERE the bee sucks there suck I :
In a cowslip's bell I lie;
There I couch, when owls do cry :
On the bat's back I do fly
After summer merrily.
Merrily, merrily, shall I live now,
Under the blossom that hangs on
the bough !

—*William Shakespeare.*

2

COME unto these yellow sands,
        And then take hands:
    Courtsied when you have, and kiss'd
        The wild waves whist,
Foot it featly here and there;
And, sweet Sprites, the burthen bear.
        Hark, hark!
        Bow-bow.
    The watch-dogs bark:
        Bow-wow.
    Hark, hark! I hear
The strain of strutting chanticleer
    Cry, Cock-a-diddle-dow!

—*William Shakespeare.*

3

FULL fathom five thy father lies:
　　Of his bones are coral made;
　Those are pearls that were his eyes:
　　Nothing of him that doth fade,
But doth suffer a sea-change
Into something rich and strange.
Sea-nymphs hourly ring his knell:
　Hark! now I hear them,—
　　Ding, dong, bell.
　　　　　　　— *William Shakespeare.*

Man and Woman

SIGH no more, ladies, sigh no more, —
　Men were deceivers ever,
　One foot in sea and one on shore,
　To one thing constant never :
—Then sigh not so, but let them go,
And be you blithe and bonny,
Converting all your sounds of woe
Into, Hey nonny, nonny.

Sing no more ditties, sing no more,
Of dumps so dull and heavy ;
　The fraud of men was ever so
　Since summer first was leafy :
— Then sigh not so, but let them go,
And be you blithe and bonny,
Converting all your sounds of woe
Into, Hey nonny, nonny.

— William Shakespeare.

Spring

WHEN daisies pied and violets blue
And lady-smocks all silver-white
And cuckoo-buds of yellow hue
Do paint the meadows with delight,
The cuckoo then, on every tree,
Mocks married men; for thus sings he,

CUCKOO;

Cuckoo, cuckoo:—O word of fear,
Unpleasing to a married ear!

When shepherds pipe on oaten straws
And merry larks are ploughmen's clocks,
When turtles tread, and rooks, and daws

[48]

And maidens bleach their summer smocks,
The cuckoo then, on every tree,
Mocks married men; for thus sings he,

Cuckoo;

Cuckoo, cuckoo:—O word of fear,
Unpleasing to a married ear!

—*William Shakespeare.*

Winter

WHEN icicles hang by the wall
   And Dick the shepherd blows his nail,
And Tom bears logs into the hall,
   And milk comes frozen home in pail;
When blood is nipt, and ways be foul,
Then nightly sings the staring owl
        Tu-whit!
  Tu-who!　A merry note!
While greasy Joan doth keel the pot.

When all about the wind doth blow,
   And coughing drowns the parson's saw,
And birds sit brooding in the snow,
   And Marian's nose looks red and raw;
When roasted crabs hiss in the bowl —
Then nightly sings the staring owl
        Tu-whit!
Tu-who!　A merry note!
While greasy Joan doth keei the pot.

                —William Shakespeare.

BLOW, blow, thou winter wind,
Thou art not so unkind
As man's ingratitude;
Thy tooth is not so keen
Because thou art not seen,
Although thy breath be rude.
Heigh ho! sing heigh ho! unto the
green holly:
Most friendship is feigning, most loving
mere folly:
Then, heigh ho! the holly!
This life is most jolly.

Freeze, freeze, thou bitter sky,
Thou dost not bite so nigh
As benefits forgot:
Though thou the waters warp,
Thy sting is not so sharp
As friend remember'd not.

Heigh ho! sing heigh ho! unto the green
   holly :
Most friendship is feigning, most loving mere
   folly :
  Then, heigh ho! the holly!
  This life is most jolly.

       — *William Shakespeare.*

UNDER the greenwood tree
　　Who loves to lie with me,
　　And turn his merry note
　　Unto the sweet bird's throat —
Come hither, come hither, come hither!
　　　　Here shall he see
　　　　No enemy
But winter and rough weather.

　　Who doth ambition shun
　　And loves to live i' the sun,
　　Seeking the food he eats
　　And pleased with what he gets —
Come hither, come hither, come hither!
　　　　Here shall he see
　　　　No enemy
But winter and rough weather.

　　　　　　　—*William Shakespeare.*

ARK! hark! the lark at heaven's gate
    sings,
   And Phœbus 'gins arise,
  His steeds to water at those springs
   On chaliced flowers that lies;
And winking May-buds begin
  To ope their golden eyes:
With everything that pretty bin,
  My lady sweet, arise;
   Arise, arise.

                 —William Shakespeare.

Fidele

FEAR no more the heat o' the sun
　　Nor the furious winter's rages;
Thou thy worldly task hast done,
　　Home art gone and ta'en thy wages:
Golden lads and girls all must,
As chimney-sweepers come to dust.

Fear no more the frown o' the great,
　　Thou art past the tyrant's stroke;
Care no more to clothe and eat;
　　To thee the reed is as the oak:
The sceptre, learning, physic, must
All follow this, and come to dust.

[57]

Fidele

Fear no more the lightning-flash
    Nor the all-dreaded thunder-stone;
Fear not slander, censure rash;
    Thou hast finish'd joy and moan:
All lovers young, all lovers must
Consign to thee, and come to dust.

— William Shakespeare.

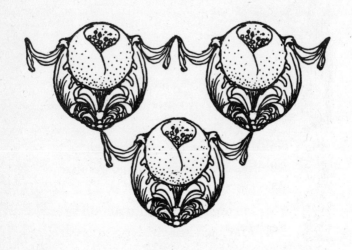

Sylvia

WHO is Sylvia? what is she,
　　That all our swains commend her?
Holy, fair, and wise is she;
　　The heaven such grace did lend her
That she might admired be.

Is she kind as she is fair?
　　For beauty lives with kindness:
Love doth to her eyes repair,
　　To help him of his blindness;
And, being help'd, inhabit there.

Then to Sylvia let us sing,
　　That Sylvia is excelling;
She excels each mortal thing
　　Upon the dull earth dwelling:
To her let us garlands bring.

　　　　　　　　　　—William Shakespeare.

[59]

O MISTRESS mine, where are you roaming?
O stay and hear! your true-love's coming
   That can sing both high and low;
Trip no further, pretty sweeting,
Journeys end in lovers meeting—
   Every wise man's son doth know.

What is love? 'tis not hereafter;
Present mirth hath present laughter;
   What's to come is still unsure:
In delay there lies no plenty,—
Then come kiss me, Sweet-and-twenty,
   Youth's a stuff will not endure.
                —*William Shakespeare.*

Song of Autolycus

WHEN daffodils begin to peer,
　　With heigh! the doxy over the dale,
Why then comes in the sweet o' the year;
　　For the red blood reigns in the winter's pale.

The white sheet bleaching on the hedge,
　　With heigh! the sweet birds, O, how they
　　　　sing!
Doth set my pugging tooth on edge;
　　For a quart of ale is a dish for a king.

The Song of Autolycus

The lark, that tirra-lyra chants,
  With heigh! with heigh! the thrush and the
      jay,
Are summer songs for me and my aunts,
  While we lie tumbling in the hay.

But shall I go mourn for that, my dear?
  The pale moon shines by night:
And when I wander here and there,
  I then do most go right.

If tinkers may have leave to live
  And bear the sow-skin budget,
Then my account I well may give
  And in the stocks avouch it.

Jog on, jog on, the foot-path way,
  And merrily hent the stile-a:
A merry heart goes all the day,
  Your sad, tires in a mile-a.

                              — *William Shakespeare.*

COME away, come away, Death,
    And in sad cypress let me be laid;
    Fly away, fly away, breath;
    I am slain by a fair cruel maid.

My shroud of white, stuck all with
       yew,
    O prepare it!
My part of death, no one so true
    Did share it.

Not a flower, not a flower sweet
On my black coffin let there be strown;
    Not a friend, not a friend greet
My poor corpse, where my bones shall be
    thrown:

A thousand thousand sighs to save,
    Lay me, O where
Sad true lover never find my grave,
    To weep there.

                    —William Shakespeare.

THAT time of year thou mayst in me
  behold
  When yellow leaves, or none, or few,
  do hang
Upon those boughs which shake against
  the cold,
Bare ruin'd choirs, where late the sweet
  birds sang:

In me thou seest the twilight of such day
As after sunset fadeth in the west,
Which by and by black night doth take away,
Death's second self, that seals up all in rest:

In me thou seest the glowing of such fire,
That on the ashes of his youth doth lie
As the death-bed whereon it must expire,
Consumed with that which it was nourish'd by:

This thou perceiv'st, which makes thy love
  more strong,
To love that well which thou must leave ere
  long.   — *William Shakespeare.*

[65]

ET me not to the marriage of true
  minds
    Admit impediments. Love is not
    love
Which alters when it alteration finds,
Or bends with the remover to re-
  move:—

O no! it is an ever-fixèd mark
That looks on tempests, and is never
  shaken;
It is the star to every wandering bark,
Whose worth's unknown, although his height
  be taken.

Love's not Time's fool, though rosy lips and
  cheeks
Within his bending sickle's compass come;

"Let me not to the marriage of true minds"

Love alters not with his brief hours and weeks,
But bears it out ev'n to the edge of doom:—

If this be error, and upon me proved,
I never writ, nor no man ever loved.

—*William Shakespeare.*

SHALL I compare thee to a summer's day?
Thou art more lovely and more temperate:
Rough winds do shake the darling buds of May,
And summer's lease hath all too short a date:

Sometime too hot the eye of heaven shines,
And often is his gold complexion dimm'd:
And every fair from fair sometime declines,
By chance, or nature's changing course, untrimm'd.

But thy eternal summer shall not fade
Nor lose possession of that fair thou owest;

Nor shall Death brag thou wanderest in his
  shade,
When in eternal lines to time thou growest: —

So long as men can breathe, or eyes can see,
So long lives this, and this gives life to thee.
— *William Shakespeare.*

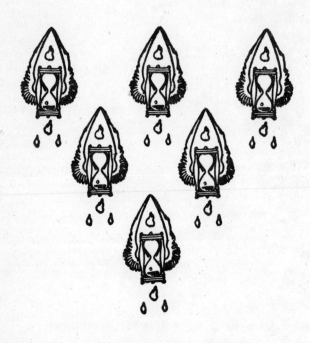

WHEN in the chronicle of wasted time
    I see descriptions of the fairest
        wights,
    And beauty making beautiful old
        rhyme
In praise of ladies dead, and lovely
    knights;

Then in the blazon of sweet beauty's
    best
Of hand, of foot, of lip, of eye, of
    brow,
I see their antique pen would have exprest
Ev'n such a beauty as you master now.

So all their praises are but prophecies
Of this our time, all, you prefiguring;

"When in the chronicle of wasted time"

And for they look'd but with divining eyes,
They had not still enough your worth to sing:

For we, which now behold these present days,
Have eyes to wonder, but lack tongues to
praise.

— *William Shakespeare.*

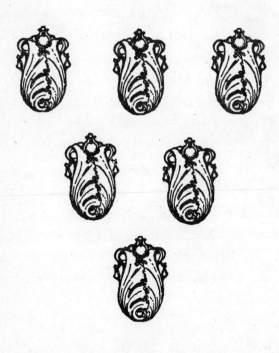

To Celia

DRINK to me only with thine eyes,
      And I will pledge with mine;
Or leave a kiss but in the cup
      And I'll not look for wine.
The thirst that from the soul doth rise
      Doth ask a drink divine;
But might I of Jove's nectar sup,
      I would not change for thine.

  I sent thee late a rosy wreath,
      Not so much honouring thee
As giving it a hope that there
      It could not wither'd be;
But thou thereon didst only breathe
      And sent'st it back to me;
Since when it grows, and smells, I swear,
      Not of itself, but thee!

                                    — *Ben Jonson.*

The Sweet Neglect

Still to be neat, still to be drest,
As you were going to a feast:
Still to be powdered, still perfumed:
Lady, it is to be presumed;
Though art's hid causes are not found,
All is not sweet, all is not sound.

Give me a look, give me a face,
That makes simplicity a grace;
Robes loosely flowing, hair as free:
Such sweet neglect more taketh me,
Than all the adulteries of art,
That strike mine eyes, but not my heart.

— *Ben Jonson.*

The Shepherds' Holiday

First Nymph.

THUS, thus begin, the yearly rites
Are due to Pan on these bright nights:
His morn now riseth and invites
To sport, to dances, and delights:
    All envious and profane, away!
    This is the shepherds' holiday.

Second Nymph.

Strew, strew the glad and smiling ground
With every flower, yet not confound;
The primrose drop, the spring's own spouse,
Bright day's-eyes, and the lips of cows,

The Shepherds' Holiday

The garden-star, the queen of May,
The rose, to crown the holiday.

Third Nymph.

Drop, drop you violets, change your hues
Now red, now pale, as lovers use,
And in your death go out as well,
As when you lived unto the smell:
That from your odour all may say,
This is the shepherds' holiday.

— *Ben Jonson.*

Echo's Song

BLOW, slow, fresh fount, keep time
with my salt tears:
  Yet slower, yet: O faintly gentle
springs:
List to the heavy part the music bears,
  Woe weeps out her division, when she
sings,
    Droop herbs and flowers,
    Fall grief in showers,
    Our beauties are not ours;
      O I could still
Like melting snow upon some craggy hill,
    Drop, drop, drop, drop,
Since nature's pride is now a withered daffodil.

—Ben Jonson.

An Ode to Himself

WHERE dost thou careless lie
    Buried in ease and sloth?
Knowledge, that sleep, doth die;
And this security,
    It is the common moth,
That eats on wits and arts, and (so)
    destroy them both.

Are all the Aonian springs
    Dried up? lies Thespia waste?
Doth Clarius' harp want strings,
That not a nymph now sings?
    Or droop they as disgraced,
To see their seats and bowers by chattering pies
    defaced?

If hence thy silence be,
    As 'tis too just a cause,
Let this thought quicken thee:

[79]

An Ode to Himself

Minds that are great and free
    Should not on fortune pause ;
Tis crown enough to virtue still, her own applause.

What though the greedy fry
    Be taken with false baits
Of worded balladry,
And think it poesy ?
    That die with their conceits,
And only piteous scorn upon their folly waits.

Then take in hand thy lyre,
    Strike in thy proper strain,
With Japhet's line aspire
Sol's chariot for new fire,
    To give the world again :
Who aided him, will thee, the issue of Jove's brain.

And since our dainty age,
    Cannot endure reproof,
Make not thyself a page,
To that strumpet the stage,
    But sing high and aloof,
Safe from the wolf's black jaw, and the dull ass's
    hoof.
               — *Ben Jonson.*

The Invitation

LIVE with me still, and all the meas-
ures
    Played to by the spheres I'll teach
    thee;
Let's but thus dally, all the pleasures
    The moon beholds her man shall reach
    thee.

Dwell in mine arms, aloft we'll hover,
    And see fields of armies fighting:
Oh, part not from me! I'll discover
There all but books of fancy's writing.

Be but my darling, Age to free thee
    From her curse shall fall a-dying;
Call me thy empress, Time to see thee
    Shall forget his art of flying.

— *Thomas Dekker.*

Good-Morrow

PACK, clouds, away, and welcome day,
    With night we banish sorrow;
Sweet air, blow soft, mount, larks,
    aloft
    To give my Love good-morrow!
Wings from the wind to please her
    mind
    Notes from the lark I'll borrow;
Bird, prune thy wing, nightingale, sing,
    To give my Love good-morrow;
    To give my Love good-morrow
    Notes from them both I'll borrow.

Wake from thy nest, Robin-red-breast,
    Sing, birds, in every furrow;
And from each hill, let music shrill
    Give my fair Love good-morrow!

Good-Morrow

Blackbird and thrush in every bush,
    Stare, linnet, and cock-sparrow!
You pretty elves, amongst yourselves
    Sing my fair Love good-morrow;
    To give my Love good-morrow
    Sing, birds, in every furrow!

                     — *Thomas Heywood.*

To Phyllis

YE little birds that sit and sing
   Amidst the shady valleys,
And see how Phyllis sweetly walks
   Within her garden alleys;
Go, pretty birds, about her bower;
Sing, pretty birds, she may not lower:
Ah me! methinks I see her frown;
   Ye pretty wantons, warble.

Go, tell her through your chirping bills
   As you by me are bidden,
To her is only known by love
   Which from the world is hidden.

GEORGE WHARTON EDWARDS

To Phyllis

Go, pretty birds, and tell her so,
See that your notes strain not too low,
For still methinks I see her frown;
   Ye pretty wantons, warble.

Go, tune your voices' harmony,
   And sing I am her lover;
Strain loud and sweet, that every note
   With sweet content may move her.
And she that hath the sweetest voice,
Tell her I will not change my choice:
Yet still methinks I see her frown;
   Ye pretty wantons, warble.

Oh fly! make haste! see, see, she falls
   Into a pretty slumber;
Sing round about her rosy bed,
   That waking she may wonder;
Say to her 'tis her lover true,
That sendeth love to you, to you;
And when you hear her kind reply,
   Return with pleasant warblings.

                              — *Thomas Heywood.*

BEAUTY clear and fair,
    Where the air
Rather like a perfume dwells;
    Where the violet and the rose
    Their blue veins in blush disclose,
And come to honour nothing else;

Where to live near,
    And planted there,
Is to live, and still live new;
    Where to gain a favour is
    More than light, perpetual bliss,—
Make me live by serving you.

Dear, again back recall
    To this light,
A stranger to himself and all.
    Both the wonder and the story
    Shall be yours, and eke the glory;
I am your servant, and your thrall.

—Beaumont and Fletcher.

[87]

Invocation to Sleep

CARE–CHARMING Sleep, thou easer
    of all woes,
    Brother to Death, sweetly thyself
      dispose
On this afflicted prince; fall like a cloud
In gentle showers; give nothing that is
    loud
Or painful to his slumbers; — easy, sweet,
And as a purling stream, thou son of
    night,
Pass by his troubled senses; sing his
    pain
Like hollow murmuring wind or silver rain;
Into this prince gently, oh, gently slide,
And kiss him into slumber like a bride!

                — *Beaumont and Fletcher.*

To Celia Singing

YOU that think love can convey
        No other way,
But through the eyes, into the heart,
        His fatal dart,
Close up those casements and but hear
        This siren sing,
        And on the wing
Of her sweet voice it shall appear
That love can enter at the ear.

Then unvail your eyes, behold
        The curious mould
Where that voice dwells, and as we know,
        When the cocks crow,
        We freely may
        Gaze on the day,
So may you when the music's done,
Awake and see the rising sun.

                — *Thomas Carew.*

Hymn to Pan

SING his praises that doth keep
  Our flocks from harm,
Pan, the father of our sheep;
  And arm in arm
Tread we softly in a round,
While the hollow neighb'ring ground
Fills the music with her sound.

Pan, O great god Pan, to thee
  Thus do we sing:
Thou that keep'st us chaste and free,
  As the young spring.
Ever be thy honour spoke,
From that place the morn is broke,
To that place day doth unyoke!

—*Beaumont and Fletcher.*

For Summer Time

Now the glories of the year
May be viewed at the best,
And the earth doth now appear
In her fairest garments drest:
 Sweetly smelling plants and flowers
 Do perfume the garden bowers;
Hill and valley, wood and field,
Mixed with pleasure profits yield.

Much is found where nothing was,
Herds on every mountain go,
In the meadows flowery grass
Makes both milk and honey flow;
 Now each orchard banquets giveth,
 Every hedge with fruit relieveth;

For Summer Time

And on every shrub and tree
Useful fruits or berries be.

Walks and ways which winter marr'd
By the winds are swept and dried;
Moorish grounds are now so hard
That on them we safe may ride:
  Warmth enough the sun doth lend us,
  From his heat the shades defend us;
And thereby we share in these
Safety, profit, pleasure, ease.

Other blessings, many more,
At this time enjoyed may be,
And in this my song therefore
Praise I give, O Lord! to Thee:
  Grant that this my free oblation
  May have gracious acceptation,
And that I may well employ
Everything which I enjoy.
             — George Wither.

The Manly Heart

SHALL I, wasting in despair,
  Die because a woman's fair?
  Or make pale my cheeks with care
  'Cause another's rosy are?
Be she fairer than the day
Or the flowery meads in May —
  If she think not well of me,
  What care I how fair she be?

Shall my silly heart be pined
'Cause I see a woman kind;
Or a well disposèd nature
Joinèd with a lovely feature?

The Manly Heart

Be she meeker, kinder, than
Turtle-dove or pelican,
    If she be not so to me,
    What care I how kind she be?

Shall a woman's virtues move
Me to perish for her love?
Or her well-deservings known
Make me quite forget mine own?
Be she with that goodness blest
Which may merit name of Best;
    If she be not such to me,
    What care I how good she be?

'Cause her fortune seems too high,
Shall I play the fool and die?
She that bears a noble mind
If not outward helps she finds,
Thinks what with them he would do
Who without them dares her woo;
    And unless that mind I see,
    What care I how great she be?

The Manly Heart

Great or good, or kind or fair,
I will ne'er the more despair;
If she love me, this believe,
I will die ere she shall grieve;
If she slight me when I woo,
I can scorn and let her go;
    For if she be not for me,
    What care I for whom she be?

— George Wither.

PHOEBUS, arise !
  And paint the sable skies
  With azure, white, and red :
  Rouse Memnon's mother from her
    Tithon's bed
That she may thy career with roses
    spread :
The nightingales thy coming each-where
    sing :
Make an eternal Spring !
Give life to this dark world which lieth
    dead ;
Spread forth thy golden hair
In larger locks than thou wast wont before,
And emperor-like decore
With diadem of pearl thy temples fair :
Chase hence the ugly night
Which serves but to make dear thy glorious
    light.

—This is that happy morn,
That day, long-wishèd day
Of all my life so dark,
(If cruel stars have not my ruin sworn
And fates my hopes betray),
Which, purely white, deserves
An everlasting diamond should it mark.
This is the morn should bring unto this grove
My Love, to hear and recompense my love.
Fair King, who all preserves,
But show thy blushing beams,
And thou two sweeter eyes
Shalt see than those which by Penèus' streams
Did once thy heart surprise.
Now, Flora, deck thyself in fairest guise:
If that ye winds would hear
A voice surpassing far Amphion's lyre,
Your furious chiding stay;
Let Zephyr only breathe,
And with her tresses play.
—The winds all silent are,
And Phœbus in his chair
Ensaffroning sea and air
Makes vanish every star:

"Phœbus, arise"

Night like a drunkard reels
Beyond the hills, to shun his flaming wheels:
The fields with flowers are deck'd in every hue,
The clouds with orient gold spangle their blue;
Here is the pleasant place —
And nothing wanting is, save She, alas!

— William Drummond of Hawthornden.

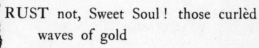

RUST not, Sweet Soul! those curlèd
    waves of gold
   With gentle tides which on your
    temples flow,
Nor temples spread with flakes of virgin
   snow,
Nor snow of cheeks with Tyrian grain
   enroll'd.
Trust not those shining lights which
   wrought my woe,
When first I did their burning rays be-
   hold;
Nor voice whose sounds more strange effects
   do show
Than of the Thracian harper have been told!
Look to this dying lily, fading rose,
Dark hyacinth, of late whose blushing beams
Made all the neighbouring herbs and grass
   rejoice

GEORGE WHARTON EDWARDS

"Trust not, Sweet Soul"

And think how little is 'twixt life's extremes!
The sweet tyrant that did kill those flowers
Shall once, ay me, not spare that Spring of
    yours.

                 — *William Drummond.*

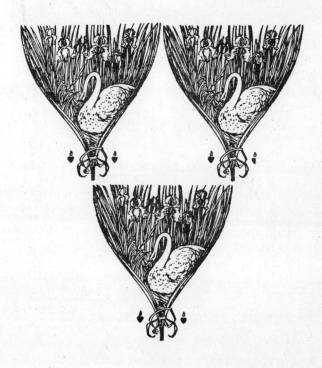

The Song of Celadyne

MARINA's gone and now sit I
  As Philomela on a thorn,
Turned out of nature's livery,
  Mirthless, alone, and all forlorn:
Only she sings not, while my sorrow can
Breathe forth such notes as suit a dying swan.

So shuts the marigold her leaves
  At the departure of the sun;
So from the honey-suckle sheaves
  The bee goes when the day is done;

The Song of Celadyne

So sits the turtle when she is but one,
And so all woe, as I, since she is gone.

To some few birds kind nature hath
   Made all the summer as one day ;
Which once enjoy'd, cold winter's wrath,
   As night, they sleeping pass away.
Those happy creatures are, they know not yet,
The pain to be deprived, or to forget.

I oft have heard men say there be
   Some, that with confidence profess
The helpful Art of Memory ;
   But could they teach forgetfulness,
I'd learn, and try what further art could do
To make me love her and forget her too.

Sad melancholy, that persuades
   Men from themselves, to think they be
Headless, or other body's shades,
   Hath long and bootless dwelt with me.
For could I think she some idea were
I still might love, forget, and have her here.

[105]

The Song of Celadyne

For such she is not; nor would I
   For twice as many torments more,
As her bereaved company
   Hath brought to those I felt before;
For then no future time might hap to know
That she deserv'd, or I did love her so.

Ye hours then, but as minutes be!
   Though so I shall be sooner old,
Till I those lovely graces see,
   Which but in her, can none behold.
Then be an age! That we may never try
More grief in parting, but grow old and die.

                    — *William Browne.*

ASK me no more where Jove bestows,
When June is past, the fading rose;
For in your beauties orient deep
These flowers, as in their causes,
sleep.

Ask me no more whither do stray
The golden atoms of the day;
For, in pure love, heaven did prepare
These powers to enrich your hair.

Ask me no more, whither doth haste
The nightingale, when May is past;
For in your sweet dividing throat
She winters, and keeps warm her note.

" Ask me no' more where Jove bestows "

Ask me no more where those stars light
That downwards fall in dead of night;
For in your eyes they sit, and there
Fixèd become, as in their sphere.

Ask me no more if east or west
The phœnix builds her spicy nest;
For unto you at last she flies,
And in your fragrant bosom dies.

— Thomas Carew.

Disdain Returned

H E that loves a rosy cheek
   Or a coral lip admires,
Or from star-like eyes doth seek
   Fuel to maintain his fires;
As old Time makes these decay,
   So his flames must waste away.

But a smooth and steadfast mind,
   Gentle thoughts, and calm desires,
Hearts with equal love combined,
   Kindle never-dying fires: —
Where these are not, I despise
   Lovely cheeks or lips or eyes.

— Thomas Carew.

Chloris in the Snow

SAW fair Chloris walk alone
When feather'd rain came softly
    down, —
    Then Jove descended from his tower
To court her in a silver shower;
The wanton snow flew to her breast,
Like little birds into their nest;
But overcome with whiteness there,
For grief it thaw'd into a tear;
Then, falling down her garment hem,
To deck her, froze into a gem.

— *Thomas Carew.*

Delight in Disorder

A SWEET disorder in the dress
Kindles in clothes a wantonness: —
A lawn about the shoulders thrown
Into a fine distractiòn, —
An erring lace, which here and there
Enthrals the crimson stomacher, —
A cuff neglectful, and thereby
Ribbands to flow confusedly, —
A winning wave, deserving note,
In the tempestuous petticoat, —
A careless shoe-string, in whose tie
I see a wild civility, —
Do more bewitch me, than when art
Is too precise in every part.

—*Robert Herrick.*

To Julia

ER lamp the glow-worm lend thee!
The shooting stars attend thee!
And the elves also,
Whose little eyes glow
Like the sparks of fire, befriend thee!

No Will-o'-the-Wisp mislight thee!
Nor snake nor slow-worm bite thee!
But on! on thy way,
Not making a stay,
Since ghost there's none to affright thee!

Let not the dark thee cumber!
What though the moon does slumber?
The stars of the night
Will lend thee their light,
Like tapers clear without number.

Then, Julia! let me woo thee
Thus, thus to come unto me:
    And when I shall meet
    Thy silvery feet,
My soul I'll pour into thee.

—Robert Herrick.

To Meadows

Yᴇ have been fresh and green,
  Ye have been filled with flowers;
And ye the walks have been
  Where maids have spent their hours.

You have beheld how they
  With wicker arks did come
To kiss and bear away
  The richer cowslips home.

You've heard them sweetly sing,
  And seen them in a round;
Each virgin, like a Spring,
  With honeysuckles crowned.

But now we see none here
  Whose silvery feet did tread
And with dishevell'd hair
  Adorn'd this smoother mead.

Like unthrifts, having spent
  Your stock, and needy grown,
You're left here to lament
  Your poor estate alone.

— Robert Herrick.

To the Virgins, to make much of Time

GATHER ye rosebuds while ye may,
　　Old Time is still a-flying:
And this same flower that smiles to-day
　　To-morrow will be dying.

The glorious lamp of heaven, the Sun,
　　The higher he's a-getting,
The sooner will his race be run,
　　And nearer he's to setting.

That age is best which is the first,
　　When youth and blood are warmer;
But being spent, the worse, and worst
　　Times, still succeed the former.

GEORGE WHARTON EDWARDS

To the Virgins, to make much of time

Then be not coy, but use your time,
  And while ye may, go marry:
For having lost but once your prime,
  You may for ever tarry.

—*Robert Herrick.*

To the Rose

G O, happy Rose, and interwove
   With other flowers, bind my Love
     Tell her too, she must not be
     Longer flowing, longer free,
     That so oft has fetter'd me.

Say, if she's fretful, I have bands
Of pearl and gold, to bind her hands:
     Tell her, if she struggle still,
     I have myrtle rods at will,
     For to tame, though not to kill.

Take thou my blessing thus, and go
And tell her this,—but do not so!—
     Lest a handsome anger fly
     Like a lightning from her eye,
     And burn thee up, as well as I.

— Robert Herrick.

To Daffodils

FAIR Daffodils, we weep to see
    You haste away so soon:
As yet the early-rising Sun
    Has not attain'd his noon.
       Stay, stay,
    Until the hasting day
       Has run
    But to the even-song;
And, having pray'd together, we
    Will go with you along.

We have short time to stay, as you,
    We have as short a Spring;
As quick a growth to meet decay
    As you, or any thing.

To Daffodils

We die,
As your hours do, and dry
Away
Like to the Summer's rain;
Or as the pearls of morning's dew
Ne'er to be found again.

— *Robert Herrick.*

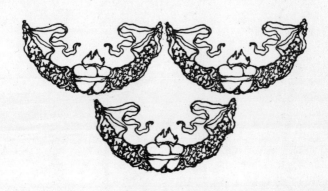

GEORGE WHARTON EDWARDS

Corinna's Maying

ET up, get up for shame! The bloom-
    ing morn
  Upon her wings presents the god
    unshorn.
  See how Aurora throws her fair
  Fresh-quilted colours through the
    air:
  Get up, sweet Slug-a-bed, and see
  The dew bespangling herb and tree.
Each flower has wept, and bow'd toward
    the east,
  Above an hour since; yet you not drest,
  Nay! not so much as out of bed?
  When all the birds have matins said,
  And sung their thankful hymns: 'tis sin,
  Nay, profanation, to keep in, —
Whenas a thousand virgins on this day,
Spring, sooner than the lark, to fetch in May.

Rise; and put on your foliage, and be seen
To come forth, like the Spring-time, fresh and
     green,
    And sweet as Flora. Take no care
    For jewels for your gown, or hair:
    Fear not; the leaves will strew
    Gems in abundance upon you:
Besides, the childhood of the day has kept,
Against you come, some orient pearls unwept:
    Come, and receive them while the light
    Hangs on the dew-locks of the night:
    And Titan on the eastern hill
    Retires himself, or else stands still
Till you come forth. Wash, dress, be brief in
     praying:
Few beads are best, when once we go a Maying.

Come, my Corinna, come; and coming, mark
How each field turns a street; each street a park
    Made green, and trimm'd with trees; see how
    Devotion gives each house a bough
    Or branch: Each porch, each door, ere this
    An ark, a tabernacle is,
Made up of white-thorn neatly interwove;

As if here were those cooler shades of love.
 Can such delights be in the street,
 And open fields, and we not see't?
 Come, we'll abroad: and let's obey
 The proclamation made for May:
And sin no more, as we have done, by staying;
But, my Corinna, come, let's go a Maying.

There's not a budding boy, or girl, this day,
But is got up, and gone to bring in May.
 A deal of youth, ere this, is come
 Back, and with white-thorn laden home.
 Some have despatch'd their cakes and cream,
 Before that we have left to dream:
And some have wept, and woo'd, and plighted
  troth,
And chose their priest, ere we can cast off sloth:
 Many a green-gown has been given;
 Many a kiss, both odd and even:
 Many a glance too has been sent
 From out the eye, Love's firmament:
Many a jest told of the keys betraying
This night, and locks pick'd:—Yet we're not
 a Maying.

Corinna's Maying

—Come, let us go, while we are in our prime;
And take the harmless folly of the time!
  We shall grow old apace, and die
  Before we know our liberty.
  Our life is short; and our days run
  As fast away as does the sun:—
And as a vapour, or a drop of rain
Once lost, can ne'er be found again:
  So when or you or I are made
  A fable, song, or fleeting shade;
  All love, all liking, all delight
  Lies drown'd with us in endless night.
Then while time serves, and we are but decaying,
Come, my Corinna! come, let's go a Maying.

—*Robert Herrick.*

To Daisies

SHUT not so soon! the dull-eyed
    Night
        Has not as yet begun,
    To make a seizure on the light
        Or to seal up the sun.

No marigolds yet closèd are,
    No shadows great appear,
Nor doth the early shepherds' star,
    Shine like a spangle here.

Stay but until my Julia close,
    Her life-begetting eye;
And let the whole world then dispose,
    Itself to live or die.
                    — *Robert Herrick.*

To Anthea who may command him Any Thing

Bɪᴅ me to live, and I will live
    Thy Protestant to be:
Or bid me love, and I will give
    A loving heart to thee.

A heart as soft, a heart as kind,
    A heart as sound and free
As in the whole world thou canst find,
    That heart I'll give to thee.

Bid that heart stay, and it will stay,
    To honour thy decree:
Or bid it languish quite away,
    And 't shall do so for thee.

To Anthea

Bid me to weep, and I will weep
  While I have eyes to see:
And having none, yet I will keep
  A heart to weep for thee.

Bid me despair, and I'll despair,
  Under that cypress tree:
Or bid me die, and I will dare
  E'en Death, to die for thee.

Thou art my life, my love, my heart,
  The very eyes of me,
And hast command of every part,
  To live and die for thee.

           — Robert Herrick.

To One saying she was Old

TELL me not Time hath played the
    thief
   Upon her beauty! my belief
    Might have been mock'd, and I have
    been
An heretic, if I had not seen,
My Mistress is still fair to me,
And now I all those graces see
That did adorn her virgin brow:
Her eye hath the same flame in's now
To kill or save,—the chemist's fire
Equally burns, so my desire;
Not any rosebud less within
Her cheek; the same snow on her chin;
Her voice that heavenly music bears
First charmed my soul, and in my ears

Did leave it trembling; her lips are
The self-same lovely twins they were;—
Often so many years I miss
No flower in all my Paradise;
Time, I despise thy rage and thee,—
Thieves do not always thrive, I see.

—James Shirley.

Description of Castara

IKE the violet, which alone
Prospers in some happy shade;
My Castara lives unknowne,
To no looser eye betray'd,
 For shee's to herselfe untrue,
 Who delights i' th' publicke view.

Such is her beauty, as no arts
Have enriched with borrowed grace,
Her high birth no pride imparts,
For she blushes in her place.
Folly boasted a glorious blood,
She is noblest being good.

Cautious, she knew never yet
What a wanton courtship meant;
Nor speaks bond to boast her wit,
In her silence eloquent.
>> Of herself survey she takes
>> But 'tweene men no difference makes.

She obeys with speedy will
Her grave parents' wise commands,
And so innocent that ill,
She nor acts, nor understands.
>> Women's feet runne still astray,
>> If once to ill they know the way.

She sails by that rocke, the court,
Where oft honour splits her mast:
And retir'dnesse thinks the port
Where her fame may anchor cast.
>> Vertue safely cannot sit
>> Where vice is enthron'd for wit.

She holds that day's pleasure best,
Where sin waits not on delight;

Without maske, or ball, or feast,
Sweetly spends a winter's night.
    O'er that darknesse, whence is thrust
    Prayer and sleepe, oft governs lust.

She her throne makes reason climbe,
While wild passions captive lie;
And each article of time
Her pure thoughts to Heaven flie:
    All her vowes religious be,
    All her love she vowes to me.

                — *William Habbington.*

On a Girdle

THAT which her slender waist con-
    fined
Shall now my joyful temples bind:
No monarch but would give his
    crown
His arms might do what this has done.

It was my Heaven's extremest sphere,
The pale which held that lovely deer:
My joy, my grief, my hope, my love
Did all within this circle move.

A narrow compass! and yet there
Dwelt all that's good, and all that's fair:
Give me but what this ribband bound,
Take all the rest the Sun goes round.

                                — *Edmund Waller.*

GO, lovely Rose!
   Tell her, that wastes her time and
      me,
  That now she knows,
When I resemble her to thee,
How sweet and fair she seems to be.

  Tell her that's young
And shuns to have her graces spied,
  That hadst thou sprung
In deserts, where no men abide,
Thou must have uncommended died.

  Small is the worth
Of beauty from the light retired:
  Bid her come forth,
Suffer herself to be desired,
And not blush so to be admired.

Then die! that she
The common fate of all things rare
    May read in thee:
How small a part of time they share
That are so wondrous sweet and fair!

    — *Edmund Waller.*

To Chloris

CHLORIS, yourself you so excel,
  When you vouchsafe to breathe
    my thought,
That like a spirit, with this spell,
  Of my own teaching, I am
    caught.

That eagle's fate and mine are one,
  Which on the shaft that made him
    die,
Espy'd a feather of his own,
  Wherewith he wont to soar so high.

Had Echo with so sweet a grace,
  Narcissus' loud complaints returned,
Not for reflection of his face,
  But of his voice, the boy had burned.

— *Edmund Waller.*

STAY, Phœbus! stay!
> The world to which you fly so
> fast,
>> Conveying day.
> From us to them, can pay your
> haste
> With no such object nor salute your
> rise,
> With no such wonder as De Morney's
> eyes.

Well does this prove
> The error of those antique books
>> Which made you move.
About the world: Her charming looks
Would fix your beams, and make it ever day,
Did not the rolling earth snatch her away.

— Edmund Waller.

To Flavia

IS not your beauty can engage
  My wary heart:
The sun, in all his pride and rage,
  Has not that art!
And yet he shines as bright as you,
If brightness could our souls subdue.

'Tis not the pretty things you say,
  Nor those you write,
Which can make Thyrsis' heart your
   prey:
  For that delight,
The graces of a well-taught mind,
In some of our own sex we find.

[143]

To Flavia

No, Flavia! 'tis your love I fear;
    Love's surest darts,
Those which so seldom fail him, are
    Headed with hearts:
Their very shadows make us yield;
Dissemble well, and win the field!

—*Edmund Waller.*

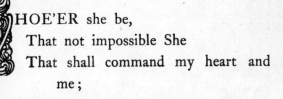

HOE'ER she be,
    That not impossible She
    That shall command my heart and
        me ;

Where'er she lie,
Lock'd up from mortal eye
In shady leaves of destiny :

Till that ripe birth
Of studied Fate stand forth,
And teach her fair steps tread our earth ;

Till that divine
Idea take a shrine
Of crystal flesh, through which to shine :

[145]

GEORGE WHARTON EDWARDS

— Meet you her, my Wishes,
Bespeak her to my blisses,
And be ye call'd, my absent kisses.

   I wish her beauty
That owes not all its duty
To gaudy tire, or glist'ring shoe-tie:

Something more than
Taffata or tissue can,
Or rampant feather, or rich fan.

A face that's best
By its own beauty drest,
And can alone commend the rest:

A face made up
Out of no other shop
Than what Nature's white hand sets ope.

Sydnæan showers
Of sweet discourse, whose powers
Can crown old Winter's head with flowers.

" Whoe'er she be "

Whate'er delight
Can make day's forehead bright
Or give down to the wings of night.

Soft silken hours,
Open suns, shady bowers;
'Bove all, nothing within that lowers.

Days, that need borrow
No part of their good morrow
From a fore-spent night of sorrow:

Days, that in spite
Of darkness, by the light
Of a clear mind are day all night.

Life, that dares send
A challenge to his end,
And when it comes, say, 'Welcome, friend.'

I wish her store
Of worth may leave her poor
Of wishes; and I wish —— no more.

"Whoe'er she be"

Now, if Time knows
That Her, whose radiant brows
Weave them a garland of my vows;

Her that dares be
What these lines wish to see:
I seek no further, it is She.

'Tis She, and here
Lo! I unclothe and clear
My wishes' cloudy character.

Such worth as this is
Shall fix my flying wishes,
And determine them to kisses.

Let her full glory,
My fancies, fly before ye;
Be ye my fictions: — but her story.

— *Richard Crashaw.*

A Ballad upon a Wedding

TELL thee, Dick, where I have
    been,
Where I the rarer things have seen;
    O, things without compare!
Such sights again cannot be found
In any place on English ground,
    Be it at wake or fair.

At Charing-Cross, hard by the way,
Where we (thou know'st) do sell our
    hay,
    There is a house with stairs;
And there did I see coming down
Such folk as are not in our town,
    Forty at least, in pairs.

A Ballad upon a Wedding

Amongst the rest, one pest'lent fine
(His beard no bigger though than thine)
    Walked on before the rest:
Our landlord looks like nothing to him:
The King (God bless him) 'twould undo him,
    Should he go still so drest.

At Course-a-Park, without all doubt,
He should have first been taken out
    By all the maids i' th' town:
Though lusty Roger there had been,
Or little George upon the Green,
    Or Vincent of the Crown.

But wot you what? the youth was going
To make an end of all his wooing:
    The parson for him stay'd:
Yet by his leave (for all his haste)
He did not so much wish all past
    (Perchance), as did the maid.

The maid (and thereby hangs a tale),
For such a maid no Whitsun-ale

A Ballad upon a Wedding

Could ever yet produce:
No grape, that's kindly ripe, could be
So round, so plump, so soft as she,
　　Nor half so full of juice.

Her finger was so small, the ring
Would not stay on, which they did bring,
　　It was too wide a peck:
And to say truth (for out it must)
It looked like the great collar (just)
　　About our young colt's neck.

Her feet beneath her petticoat,
Like little mice, stole in and out,
　　As if they fear'd the light:
And O, she dances such a way!
No sun upon an Easter-day
　　Is half so fine a sight.

Her cheeks so rare a white was on,
No daisy makes comparison,
　　(Who sees them is undone,)
For streaks of red were mingled there,

A Ballad upon a Wedding

Such as are on a Cathering pear
    The side that's next the sun.

Her lips were red, and one was thin,
Compar'd to that was next her chin
    (Some bee had stung it newly);
But, Dick, her eyes so guard her face,
I durst no more upon them gaze
    Than on the sun in July.

Her mouth so small, when she does speak,
Thou'dst swear her teeth her words did break,
    That they might passage get;
But she so handled still the matter,
They came as good as ours, or better,
    And are not spent a whit.

Just in the nick the cook knocked thrice,
And all the waiters in a trice
    His summons did obey;
Each serving-man, with dish in hand,
Marched boldly up, like our trained band,
    Presented, and away.

A Ballad upon a Wedding

When all the meat was on the table,
What man of knife or teeth was able
    To stay to be entreated?
And this the very reason was,
Before the parson could say grace,
    The company was seated.

The business of the kitchen's great,
For it is fit that men should eat;
    Nor was it then denied:
Passion o' me, how I run on!
There's that that would be thought upon
    (I trow) besides the bride.

Now hats fly off, and youths carouse;
Healths first go round, and then the house,
    The bride's came thick and thick:
And when 'twas named another's health,
Perhaps he made it hers by stealth;
    And who could help it, Dick?

On the sudden up they rise and dance;
Then sit again and sigh and glance:

A Ballad upon a Wedding

They dance again and kiss:
Thus several ways the time did pass,
Whilst ev'ry woman wished her place,
And every man wished his.

— Sir John Suckling.

WHY so pale and wan, fond lover?
    Prythee, why so pale?
Will, if looking well can't move her,
    Looking ill prevail?
    Prythee, why so pale?

Why so dull and mute, young sinner?
    Prythee, why so mute?
Will, when speaking well can't win her,
    Saying nothing do't?
    Prythee, why so mute?

Quit, quit, for shame! this will not move,
    This cannot take her;
If of herself she will not love,
    Nothing can make her:
    The D—l take her!

— Sir John Suckling.

Constancy

OUT upon it, I have loved
    Three whole days together;
And am like to love thee more,
    If it proves good weather.

Time shall moult away his wings,
    Ere he shall discover
In the whole wide world again
    Such a constant lover.

But the spite on't is, no praise
    Is due at all to me:
Love with me had made no stays,
    Had it any been but she.

Had it any been but she,
    And that very face,
There had been at least ere this
    A dozen dozen in her place.

— *Sir John Suckling.*

"I prithee send me back my heart"

PRITHEE send me back my heart,
 Since I cannot have thine:
For if from yours you will not part,
 Why then shouldst thou have
  mine?

Yet now I think on't, let it lie;
 To find it were in vain,
For thou'st a thief in either eye
 Would steal it back again.

Why should two hearts in one breast lie,
 And not yet lodge together?

"I prithee send me back my heart"

O Love! where is thy sympathy,
  If thus our breasts thou sever?

For love is such a mystery,
  I cannot find it out:
For when I think I'm best resolved,
  I then am in most doubt.

Then farewell care, and farewell woe,
  I will no longer pine;
For I'll believe I have her heart
  As much as she has mine.

—Sir John Suckling.

To Althea from Prison

WHEN Love with unconfinèd wings
   Hovers within my gates,
And my divine Althea brings
   To whisper at the grates;
When I lie tangled in her hair
   And fetter'd to her eye,
The Gods that wanton in the air
   Know no such liberty.

When flowing cups run swiftly round
   With no allaying Thames,
Our careless heads with roses bound,
   Our hearts with loyal flames;
When thirsty grief in wine we steep,
   When healths and draughts go free —
Fishes that tipple in the deep
   Know no such liberty.

To Althea from Prison

When, (like committed linnets), I
   With shriller throat shall sing
The sweetness, mercy, majesty
   And glories of my King;
When I shall voice aloud how good
   He is, how great should be,
Enlarged winds, that curl the flood,
   Know no such liberty.

Stone walls do not a prison make,
   Nor iron bars a cage;
Minds innocent and quiet take
   That for an hermitage;
If I have freedom in my love
   And in my soul am free,
Angels alone, that soar above,
   Enjoy such liberty.

— Richard Lovelace.

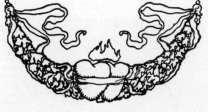

To Lucasta, going beyond the Seas

I F to be absent were to be
　　Away from thee;
　Or that when I am gone
　You or I were alone;
　Then, my Lucasta, might I crave
Pity from blustering wind, or swallowing
　　wave.

But I'll not sigh one blast or gale
　　To swell my sail,
　Or pay a tear to 'suage
　The foaming blue-god's rage;
　For whether he will let me pass
Or no, I'm still as happy as I was.

Though seas and land betwixt us both,
　　Our faith and troth,

To Lucasta, going beyond the Seas

    Like separated souls,
    All time and space controls:
  Above the highest sphere we meet
Unseen, unknown, and greet as Angels greet.

    So then we do anticipate
      Our after-fate
    And are alive i' the skies,
    If thus our lips and eyes
  Can speak like spirits unconfined
In Heaven, their earthly bodies left behind.

                    — Richard Lovelace.

To Lucasta, on going to the Wars

ELL me not, Sweet, I am unkind
   That from the nunnery
Of thy chaste breast and quiet mind,
   To war and arms I fly.

True, a new mistress now I chase,
   The first foe in the field ;
And with a stronger faith embrace
   A sword, a horse, a shield.

Yet this inconstancy is such
   As you too shall adore ;
I could not love thee, Dear, so much,
   Loved I not Honour more.

               — Richard Lovelace.

The Grasshopper

O H, thou that swing'st upon the waving
    ear
    Of some well-fillèd oaten beard,
    Drunk every night with some de-
    licious tear
    Dropt thee from heaven where thou
    wert reared:

    The joys of earth and air are thine en-
    tire,
    That with thy feet and wings dost hop
    and fly,
And when thy poppy works, thou dost retire,
To thy carved acorn-bed to lie.

Up with the day, the Sun thou welcom'st then,
    Sport'st in the gilt plaits of his beams,
And all these merry days mak'st merry men,
    Thyself, and melancholy streams.

But ah, the sickle! golden ears are cropped;
  Ceres and Bacchus bid good night;
Sharp frosty fingers all your flowers have
    topped,
  And what scythes spared, winds shave off
    quite.

— *Richard Lovelace.*

Cherry Ripe

THERE is a Garden in her face,
Where Roses and white Lilies grow;
A heav'nly paradise is that place,
Wherein all pleasant fruits do flow.
There Cherries grow which none may buy
Till Cherry ripe themselves do cry.

Those Cherries fairly do enclose
Of Orient Pearl a double row;
Which when her lovely laughter shows,
They look like Rose-buds fill'd with snow.
Yet them nor Peer nor Prince can buy
Till Cherry ripe themselves do cry.

Cherry Ripe

Her Eyes like Angels watch them still;
Her Brows like bended bows do stand,
Threatning with piercing frowns to kill
All that attempt, with eye or hand,
Those sacred Cherries to come nigh,
Till Cherry ripe themselves do cry.

— *Thomas Campion.*

THOUGH you are young, and I am
      old,
  Though your veins hot, and my
      blood cold,
Though youth is moist, and age is dry;
Yet embers live, when flames do die.

The tender graft is easily broke,
But who shall shake the sturdy Oak?
You are more fresh and fair than I;
Yet stubs do live, when flowers do die.

Thou, that thy youth dost vainly boast,
Know buds are soonest nipt with frost:
Think that thy fortune still doth cry,
Thou fool, to-morrow thou must die!

                    — Thomas Campion.

Amarillis

I CARE not for these Ladies,
  That must be wooed and prayed:
  Give me kind Amarillis,
  The wanton country maid.
Nature art disdaineth,
Her beauty is her own.
  Her when we court and kiss,
  She cries, Forsooth, let go:
  But when we come where comfort is
  She never will say No.

If I love Amarillis,
  She gives me fruit and flowers:
  But if we love these Ladies,
  We must give golden showers.
Give them gold that sell love,
Give me the Nut-brown lass,

Amarillis

Who, when we court and kiss,
She cries, Forsooth, let go:
But when we come where comfort is,
She never will say No.

These Ladies must have pillows,
And beds by strangers wrought;
Give me a Bower of willows,
Of moss and leaves unbought,
And fresh Amarillis,
With milk and honey fed;
  Who, when we court and kiss,
  She cries, Forsooth, let go:
  But when we come where comfort is,
  She never will say No!

— *Thomas Campion.*

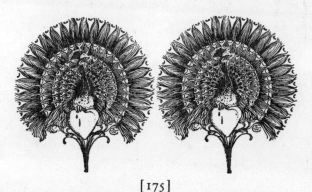

HERE she her sacred bower adorns,
The Rivers clearly flow;
The groves and meadows swell with
flowers
The winds all gently blow.
Her Sun-like beauty shines so fair,
Her Spring can never fade:
Who then can blame the life that strives
To harbour in her shade?

Her grace I sought, her love I wooed,
Her love though I obtain;
No time, no toil, no vow, no faith,
Her wishèd grace can gain.

" Where she her sacred bower adorns "

Yet truth can tell my heart is hers,
   And her will I adore;
And from that love when I depart,
   Let heav'n view me no more!

Her roses with my praise shall spring;
   And when her trees I praise,
Their boughs shall blossom, mellow fruit
   Shall strew her pleasant ways.
The words of hearty zeal have power
   High wonders to effect;
O why should then her princely ear
   My words, or zeal, neglect?

If she my faith misdeems, or worth,
   Woe worth my hapless fate!
For though time can my truth reveal,
   That time will come too late.
And who can glory in the worth,
   That cannot yield him grace?
Content, in ev'rything is not,
   Nor joy in ev'ry place.

[177]

But from her bower of Joy since I
   Must now excluded be,
And she will not relieve my cares,
   Which none can help but she;
My comfort in her love shall dwell,
   Her love lodge in my breast,
And though not in her bower, yet I
   Shall in her temple rest.

— Thomas Campion.

THE man of life upright,
  Whose guiltless heart is free
From all dishonest deeds,
  Or thought of vanity;

The man whose silent days,
  In harmless joys are spent,
Whom hopes cannot delude
  Nor sorrow discontent;

That man needs neither towers
  Nor armour for defence,
Nor secret vaults to flie
  From thunder's violence;

"The man of life upright"

He only can behold
   With unaffrighted eyes
The horrors of the deep
   The terrors of the skies.

Thus, scorning all the cares
   That fate or fortune brings,
He makes the heav'n his book,
   His wisdom heav'nly things;

Good thoughts his only friends,
   His wealth a well-spent age,
The earth his sober Inn
   And quiet Pilgrimage.

          — Thomas Campion.

THE peaceful western wind
　　The winter storms hath tam'd,
And nature in each kind
　　The kind heat hath inflam'd:
The forward buds so sweetly breathe
　　Out of their earthy bowers,
That heav'n which views their pomp
　　　beneath,
　　Would fain be deckt with flowers.

See how the morning smiles
　　On her bright eastern hill,
And with soft steps beguiles
　　Them that lie slumbring still!
The music-loving birds are come
　　From cliffs and rocks unknown,
To see the trees and briers bloom
　　That late were overflown.

"The peaceful western wind"

What Saturn did destroy,
Love's Queen revives again;
And now her naked boy
Doth in the fields remain,
Where he such pleasing change doth view
In every living thing,
As if the world were born anew
To gratify the Spring.

If all things life present,
Why die my comforts then?
Why suffers my content?
Am I the worst of men?
O beauty, be not thou accus'd
Too justly in this case!
Unkindly if true love be us'd,
'Twill yield thee little grace.

— *Robert Campion.*

MY sweetest Lesbia, let us live and
love:
And though the sager sort our deeds
reprove,
Let us not way them: heaven's great
lamps do dive
Into their west, and straight again re-
vive;
But soon as once set is our little light,
Then must we sleep one ever-during
night.

If all would lead their lives in love like me,
Then bloody swords and armour should not
be;
No drum nor trumpet peaceful sleeps should
move,

GEORGE WHARTON EDWARDS.

Unless alar'me came from the camp of love:
But fools do live, and waste their little
  light,
And seek with pain their ever-during night.

When timely death my life and fortune ends,
Let not my hearse be vext with mourning
  friends;
But let all lovers, rich in triumph, come
And with sweet pastimes grace my happy
  tomb:
And, Lesbia, close up thou my little light,
And crown with love my ever-during night.

—Robert Campion.

NIGHT as well as brightest day hath
her delight,
Let us then with mirth and music
deck the night.
Never did glad day such store
Of joy to night bequeath:
Her Stars then adore,
Both in Heav'n, and here beneath.

Love and beauty, mirth and music yield
true joys,
Though the cynics in their folly count them
toys.
Raise your spirits ne'er so high,
They will be apt to fall:
None brave thoughts envy,
Who had ere brave thought at all.

Joy is the sweet friend of life, the nurse of
      blood,
Patron of all health, and fountain of all good :
Never may joy hence depart,
   But all your thoughts attend ;
Nought can hurt the heart,
   That retains so sweet a friend.

                — *Robert Campion.*

Finis